50 Nifty
Super Scary
Crafts and Other Things to Do

Look for these other haunting titles by
Lowell House Juvenile

Scary Origami

Draw Scary

Scary Story Starters

Very Scary Dictionary

Graveyard Jokes

50 Nifty Super Scary Crafts and Other Things to Do

Written by Alison Bell
Illustrated by Will Suckow

Lowell House
Juvenile
Los Angeles

CONTEMPORARY BOOKS
Chicago

Publisher: Jack Artenstein
Associate Publisher, Juvenile Division: Elizabeth Amos
Director of Publishing Services: Rena Copperman
Managing Editor, Juvenile Division: Lindsey Hay
Editor in Chief, Juvenile Division Nonfiction: Amy Downing
Art Director: Lisa Theresa Lenthall
Editorial Assistant: Inga Herrmann
Cover Photograph: Ann Bogart
Cover Craft: Charlene Olexiewicz

Library of Congress Catalog Card Number: 96-2983

ISBN: 1-56565-540-0

Lowell House books can be purchased at special discounts when ordered in bulk for premiums and special sales. Contact Department JH at the following address:

Lowell House Juvenile
2029 Century Park East, Suite 3290
Los Angeles, CA 90067

Manufactured in the United States of America

10 9 8 7 6 5 4 3 2 1

Contents

BEFORE YOU START ...
READ THIS!

Whether you're planning a frightfully fun masquerade party, making a creepy Halloween costume, or filling a rainy evening with games for your friends, *50 Nifty Super Scary Crafts and Other Things to Do* will become your most priceless possession. In just moments you can make everything you need to transform yourself from a charming child into a terrifying presence.

These creepy concoctions will inspire the monster in you. Make a Slime-ade Stand, complete with floating eyeball ice cubes to serve your customers. Or send your siblings a ghoulish pop-out greeting card. For that extra-special someone, try Blood-Spattered Gift Wrap to decorate a truly unique gift.

Whether you're making a costume, sure to terrify the neighborhood or learning the fine art of scary storytelling, you won't want to put this book down until you've tried all fifty scary projects and activities!

The tombstone in the upper right-hand corner of each activity or craft indicates level of difficulty—1 is easiest, 3 is hardest.

Terrifying Tips for Your Creepy Crafts

On Getting Started

- Read the directions through one time to make sure you understand the project. Then refer to the instructions often while you're building the craft.

- Make sure you have all the required ingredients before you start working.

- Always ask permission to use the materials, especially if you need to rip up a sheet or cut a shirt—you want your parents to scream in fright, not anger!

- Find a clear, open space where you can create without disturbing your family or making a horrifying mess.

On Safety

- Before you paint your face with face paint, make sure to test it on your skin to see if you are allergic to it. If it itches or stings, use a different type of face paint.

- When you need to use a sharp object such as a knife, *always* ask an adult for help.

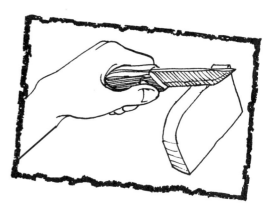

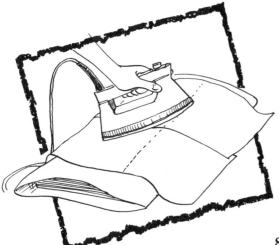

- *Always* ask an adult to help you when you need to light a candle or use any other hot object, such as an iron.

- If you have long hair, make sure to tie it back before painting, cutting, or lighting candles.

On Painting

- When painting, wear old clothing that won't be ruined if you splatter them.

- Use slow, steady strokes when painting to get an even texture.

On Cleaning

- Try to keep your monstrous mess under control by covering your work area with newspaper.

- Wipe up spills and throw away trash and newspapers as soon as you're done with them.

- Return things to where you found them, so they will be easy to find the next time you want to make a craft.

GREETING CARDS FROM BEYOND THE GRAVE

These pop-up creepy cards will send gory greetings to your faraway friends.

ICKY INGREDIENTS

• several sheets of white construction paper • fine-tipped felt pens, various colors • pencil • scissors • cellophane tape or glue • paper clips

DREADFUL DIRECTIONS

1. Fold an 8 ½-by-11-inch piece of white construction paper in half, making it a 4 ¼-by-5 ½-inch card.

2. Draw a tombstone on the outside of the card with a felt pen. In the center of the tombstone, write the name of the friend to whom you are sending the card. Or write in a creepy saying, such as "I Dare You to Open This!" (See the illustration on page 11.)

3. Decorate the inside of the card by using felt-tipped pens to draw a graveyard or another creepy setting for your pop-up monster. While you're drawing, be sure to leave space for your monster, which you will add in step 7.

4. Write a witty note inside, such as "Things have sure been dead around here since you left" or "Wish there were a ghost of a chance of seeing you soon." You can make your message anything you want.

5. Set your card aside while you create your pop-up monster. It can be a skull or any other graveyard groupie. With a pencil, draw the creature on a separate piece of white construction paper. Make sure it's small enough to fit inside the card. Color your drawing, then cut it out.

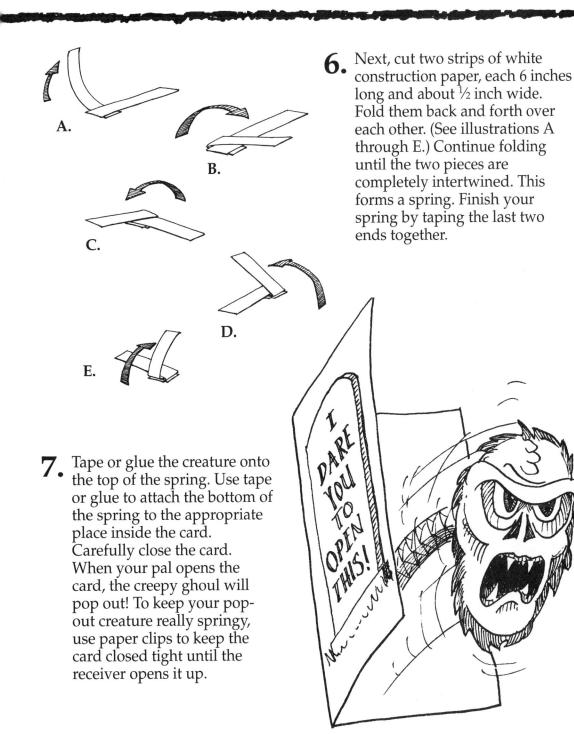

A.

B.

C.

D.

E.

6. Next, cut two strips of white construction paper, each 6 inches long and about ½ inch wide. Fold them back and forth over each other. (See illustrations A through E.) Continue folding until the two pieces are completely intertwined. This forms a spring. Finish your spring by taping the last two ends together.

7. Tape or glue the creature onto the top of the spring. Use tape or glue to attach the bottom of the spring to the appropriate place inside the card. Carefully close the card. When your pal opens the card, the creepy ghoul will pop out! To keep your pop-out creature really springy, use paper clips to keep the card closed tight until the receiver opens it up.

I DARE YOU TO OPEN THIS!

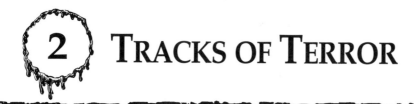

2 TRACKS OF TERROR

Who says monsters don't exist? Freak out your friends with these creepy goblin footsteps that lead beyond the grave.

ICKY INGREDIENTS

• magic marker • two big sponges (½ inch thick) • scissors • two colors of any washable paint (such as tempera paint) • two aluminum baking trays (found in any market)

DREADFUL DIRECTIONS

1. With the magic marker, draw a ferocious-looking foot on each sponge. Draw a left foot and a right foot. Add long, pointy toes to each foot.

2. Cut out the feet.

3. Now you're ready to make monster prints! Select a creepy color for each foot. Some colors to consider are blood red, ghoulish green, and beastly black. Pour each color of paint about ⅛ inch deep into an aluminum baking pan.

4. Dip each sponge into the desired paint and begin stamping your tracks of terror on a sidewalk or fence. Don't forget to alternate left and right feet as you take each "step."

FURTHER FRIGHT

With your parents' permission, "walk" your monster feet on your bedroom wall, making the tracks lead into your closet. It will look like a ghoul is lurking inside!

SHRUNKEN HEAD PEN DECORATORS

3

PARENTAL SUPERVISION RECOMMENDED
These grotesque apple apparitions will make your friends
"shrink" with revulsion!

ICKY INGREDIENTS

• small apple • sharp paring knife • two cloves • a few grains of uncooked white rice • pen

DREADFUL DIRECTIONS

1. With a parent's help, carefully peel the skin off the apple with a paring knife.

2. Leave the stem on the apple—it will be the shrunken head's single strand of hair! Use the knife to carve out a face on one side of the apple, making sure the stem is on top of the head. Carve a triangle for each eye and the nose. Carve a slit for the mouth wide enough to fit a grain of rice vertically. Your cuts should be at least ¼ inch deep.

3. Push a clove into each eye socket for the beady little eyeballs, and insert the grains of rice vertically into the mouth slit for teeth.

4. Push the dull end of a pen into the bottom of the apple. Push the pen up high enough so it won't fall out.

5. Put the apple in a warm, dry place, such as a kitchen shelf near the stove, for three to four weeks to let it dry out. Every few days, turn the apple over to make sure it doesn't rot. As the apple dries, it will harden and shrink to half its size. And, best of all, the face will look super scary.

6. Once the apple is completely dry and hard to the touch, your shrunken head pen decorator is ready. You can tell people that *this* is what happened to the last guy who didn't return your pen!

4 GREEN GOBLIN LANTERNS

PARENTAL SUPERVISION REQUIRED
When it comes to casting spooky shadows on the wall,
nothing can hold a candle to these creepy candleholders!

ICKY INGREDIENTS

• large green pepper • sharp paring knife • cutting board
• medium-sized spoon • dark-colored marker • one green
birthday candle

DREADFUL DIRECTIONS

1. With your parents' help, place the green pepper on a cutting board and carefully cut off the top of the pepper. Make the hole on top only big enough for you to get in a spoon.

2. Use the spoon to scoop out the inside of the pepper. You may need to use a knife to get out all the seeds.

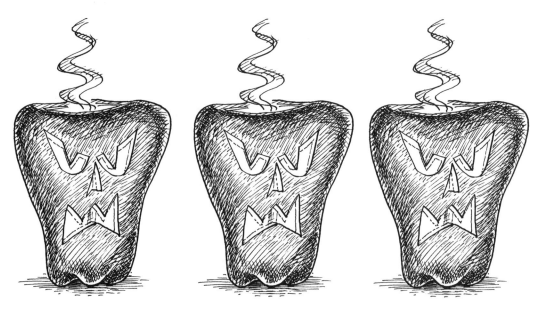

3. With a dark-colored marker, draw a goblin face on one side of the pepper. The creepier the expression, the better! With the help of a parent, you are now ready to carve out the face. Move the knife carefully along the lines you drew. Remove each pepper piece as you cut it out.

4. Make a small indentation on the bottom of the inside of the pepper to hold the candle. You don't want to cut through the pepper skin, so don't carve too deep.

5. Place the small candle in the bottom of the pepper. If the candle is too tall to fit inside the pepper, have an adult light the candle and let it burn down, then blow out the flame and put it inside. Carefully re-light the candle.

6. Scare yourself silly by dimming the lights and telling ghost stories by the ghoulish light of your green goblin lantern!

FURTHER FRIGHT

Make a whole collection of creepy lanterns for your next ghoulish party! Try using red bell peppers and mini-squash for the faces. You'll get goblins in every shape and size. Then at the end of your party, you may want to give a lantern to each guest to "light" his or her way home.

Remember, candles should be lit *only* under an adult's supervision!

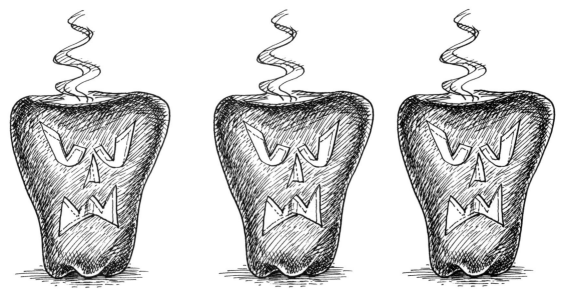

15

This flying saucer flies through the air like a Frisbee! Start a battle beyond the stars by launching this invading spaceship filled with hostile aliens.

ICKY INGREDIENTS

• three large two-ply paper plates • glue • small (12 oz.) paper bowl • black poster paint • paintbrush • sheet of white construction paper • scissors • three red ribbons, about 3 feet long each • cellophane tape

DREADFUL DIRECTIONS

1. Stack and glue three large paper plates together. By gluing the plates together, your flying saucer will have the weight it needs to fly.

2. Glue the small paper bowl upside down onto the underside of the bottom plate (the side you don't eat on). Your creation is starting to look like a spaceship already, isn't it?

3. Paint the entire spaceship with black poster paint. Add portholes to your spaceship by cutting ten circles out of the white paper. Glue them and place them evenly around the bowl.

4. Now add a shimmery rocket tail to the back of the ship! Tape three 3-foot-long pieces of red ribbon, one right next to the other, underneath the edge of the saucer.

5. Go outside with a friend and throw the saucer back and forth as you would a Frisbee. Pretend your TFO is filled with terrifying, creepy aliens just waiting to conquer the Earth!

HAUNTED HANDWRITING TREASURE HUNT

Ghosts are invisible, and so are these notes that will send your friends on a mystery-message treasure hunt.

ICKY INGREDIENTS

• white paper • thick white candle • pen • pencil • treasure

DREADFUL DIRECTIONS

1. Select a treasure hunt route to send a group of your friends on. You might send them around your neighborhood or in your house or backyard. Come up with at least five places for the treasure seekers to search.

2. Create a clue for each stop on the journey. Each clue needs to describe the place where the *next* clue can be found. For instance, if the hunt is in your house, you may give them a clue to lead them to the kitchen. Then, in the kitchen is a clue leading everyone to the living room, and so on.

3. Write down each clue on a sheet of paper using the end of a white candle to create "invisible ink." You may find it easier to draw a picture of each place the kids should go. Also, number your clues with a regular pen so you'll be able to tell which clue belongs where!

4. Before anyone arrives, put your clues in place. The clues don't have to be in plain sight, but if they're too hard to find, your pals may not find the treasure!

5. Hide a treasure at the final stop. Think of a treasure that everyone can enjoy, such as a big cake shaped like a creepy ghoul.

6. Gather your friends and start them off with the first clue. Give them one pencil, the weapon for reading the clues. Explain that when they find each piece of paper containing a clue, they need to softly rub the side of the pencil lead back and forth over the paper until the haunted handwriting magically appears!

7 THE ACCIDENT-PRONE MUMMY

Create a mummy that's so wrapped up, it can't see where it's going!

ICKY INGREDIENTS

- snug-fitting light-colored clothing • one or two old white sheets
- scissors • safety pins • Ace bandage • brightly colored scarf
- red paint • paintbrush • white powder • black eyebrow pencil
- white gloves

DREADFUL DIRECTIONS

1. Since your mummy costume will hug you tightly, wear light-colored clothes that aren't bulky, like a turtleneck and leggings or long underwear.

2. With a parent's permission, cut up a white sheet lengthwise into strips about 4 inches wide each.

3. Have a friend wrap a strip around each of your ankles and work up. Don't have him or her wrap too tightly around your knees or you won't be able to bend your legs to walk! Each strip should be either tied securely to the strip next to it or held in place with safety pins.

4. When your friend reaches your head, make sure that he or she leaves your face free. If you run out of strips, you may need to cut up another sheet. Be sure to check with a parent first!

5. Wrap an Ace bandage around your "sprained ankle." Fold a brightly colored scarf into a triangular bandage, and tie it around your neck to make a sling. Stick your "broken arm" into the scarf.

6. Add red paint to a strip for a bloody wound, and wrap it around your head. Powder your face white. With an eyebrow pencil, draw some scary scars on your face. Once you put on a pair of white gloves, you're set! Who's really behind that costume? Mum's the word!

8 BLOOD-SPATTERED GIFT WRAP

Wrap up any ghoulish gifts with this "bloodstained" paper.

ICKY INGREDIENTS

• newspaper • white craft paper (available at craft stores) • red tempera paint • small bowl • eyedropper • bandages • gauze

DREADFUL DIRECTIONS

1. First, spread out a few newspapers over your work surface to keep the paint from getting on the floor or furniture.

2. Spread out the white craft paper over the newspaper. Then, pour the red tempera paint into a small bowl.

3. You are now ready to "attack" your gift wrap! Dip an eyedropper into the bowl, and fill it with paint. Hold the dropper over the paper and shake it gently to release drops of "blood." Make sure not to squeeze the bulb of the eyedropper, otherwise you'll release all the paint at once and have a big mess on your hands! When the eyedropper runs out of paint, refill it and repeat until you think the paper is spattered enough. Let the paint dry completely.

4. Once the paint dries, you can wrap up your packages with the paper. Use bandages to tape the paper to the box, and use strips of gauze for ribbons. Just hope that your gift recipients are brave enough to open up the presents!

FURTHER FRIGHT

Add bullet holes to your paper by drawing small black holes with a marker. With a paintbrush, brush on some red paint so it looks like blood is leaking out of the bullet holes!

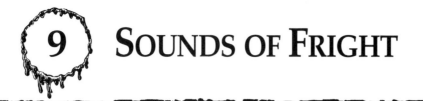

9 SOUNDS OF FRIGHT

No ghost story would be complete without scary sound effects. Tape these nightmarish noises for unlimited nights of fright.

ICKY INGREDIENTS

• paper • pencil • blank tape • tape recorder • soft-drink bottle
• TV set and remote control • table • lightweight poster board
• rice • aluminum pan • cellophane • nails • tin can

DREADFUL DIRECTIONS

1. Using paper and a pencil, write down a ghost story, either one you've heard or one you've made up.

2. Write down all the sound effects you can think of that would add to your story. Look at the list on the next page for scary sounds that are easy to create.

3. Search the house for the items you need to imitate the scary sounds you've chosen. Some of them are listed under the Icky Ingredients. These items will serve as your sound-effects props.

4. Place the sound-effects props in the order you will need them. Read your ghost story aloud to yourself a few times, incorporating the sound effects to make sure the story flows.

5. When you're ready, put a blank tape in the tape recorder and record your scary sounds. Put a one- or two-second pause in between each sound. Now you're ready to frighten your friends!

6. Invite your pals over, have everyone sit in a circle, and turn down the lights. Before you start, make sure the tape is rewound to the beginning. Then tell your ghost story, turning on the tape recorder at the appropriate times, and watch your friends squeal with delight!

POSSIBLE SCARY SOUND EFFECTS:

- For ghostly moans, blow softly over the top of a large soft-drink bottle.
- For alien voices, turn on your TV, then hold your finger down on the channel clicker. The snippets of sound from the different channels sound like garbled space creature speech. (Check with your parents for their okay on this one.)
- For monster footsteps, pound your palms, one by one, on a table or other hard surface.
- For terrifying thunder, rattle a sheet of lightweight poster board.
- For pounding rain, pour or sprinkle rice into an aluminum pan.
- For raging fires, crinkle cellophane.
- For rattling chains, shake a handful of nails in a big tin can.
- For tortured screams . . . just scream! The shriller the better!

PARENTAL SUPERVISION RECOMMENDED
Make no bones about it, this skull stamp is frighteningly fun to use.

ICKY INGREDIENTS

• paper • pencil • sharp paring knife • large potato • stamp pads in different colors (available at stationery stores)

DREADFUL DIRECTIONS

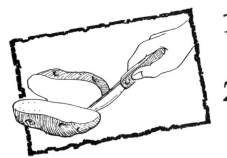

1. First, sketch a small skull on a piece of paper. With your parent's help, cut a large potato in half lengthwise.

2. Using your sketch as a guide, have a parent help you carve the outline of a skull onto one of the cut potato halves with a paring knife. Make your incisions at least an inch deep.

3. Cut away the rest of the potato to make the shape of the skull stand out. Make the skull at least an inch thick, so you have something to hold onto when you stamp.

4. Press the skull into the stamp pad and stamp away on book covers, stationery, envelopes, and any other pieces of paper that need an extra skeletal touch. Make another stamp out of the other potato half. Don't forget: these potato stamps don't last forever. You should throw them out after using.

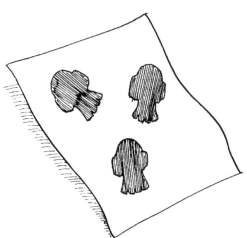

FURTHER FRIGHT

Decorate your stamped skulls with markers. Add eyes, a mouth, even hair!

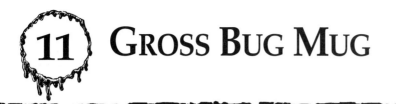

11 GROSS BUG MUG

This spider mug filled with gross, buglike goodies is the perfect gift for friends—at least those with strong stomachs!

ICKY INGREDIENTS

• paper • pencil • white ceramic mug • paint markers or other permanent (not water soluble) markers • chocolate raisins and nuts • gummy worms • white thread or string

DREADFUL DIRECTIONS

1. On a piece of paper, sketch a spider and a spiderweb. To see how your design will look on the mug, wrap the sketch around the mug, then take it off and make adjustments as needed. Once you've perfected your drawing, sketch it in pencil on your mug. If the mug does not show pencil marks, you'll have to go straight to paint markers.

2. Paint your design on the mug using the paint markers. Set it aside while it dries.

3. Fill the mug with all the crawly creatures your spider has snared: chocolate raisins, chocolate-covered nuts, and any other buglike edibles you can think of. Hang a few gummy worms over the side of the mug.

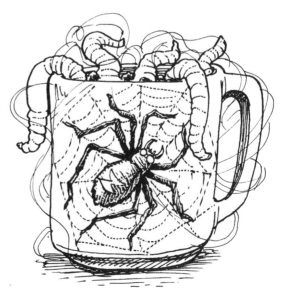

4. To finish your mug, wrap white thread or string around it to create a creepy "web." This will make it look like the spider tried to hide its yummy stash of "bugs."

12 PARTS ARE PARTS!

With this T-shirt, you can wear your favorite body parts for everyone to see!

ICKY INGREDIENTS

• paper • pencil • scissors • patches of colored felt • pen or felt-tip marker • different-colored thread • sewing needle • old nylons, tissue, or cotton balls • T-shirt • safety pins• red fabric paint • thin paintbrush

---

DREADFUL DIRECTIONS

1. Sketch a stomach, heart, and liver on a piece of paper and cut out each body part. These will be your patterns. If you're not sure what these organs look like, use the drawings as a guide. (The drawings are not actual size. You can make the organs any size you want!)

2. Place each pattern on the color of felt of your choice. (Be daring—do a green heart, yellow stomach, and blue liver!) Trace around each pattern with a pen or marker, then cut it out of the felt. You will need two pieces of felt for each organ.

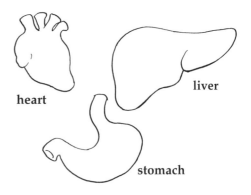

heart

liver

stomach

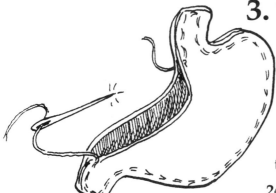

3. Choose a color of thread that matches the first organ. Thread the needle and tie a knot in the end of the thread. You may want to ask a parent or older sibling to help you with this step. Now sew the two pieces of the organ together, making your stitches about ¼ inch from the edge. Leave 4 inches open, and don't tie off the thread just yet.

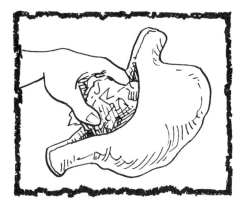

4. Turn your sewed-up organ inside out, then stuff old nylons, tissue, or cotton balls into the hole until the organ looks lifelike. Close the organ and sew up the remaining 4 inches. Tie off the thread.

5. Repeat steps 3 and 4 for each organ.

6. Ever heard of wearing your heart on a sleeve? Now you can, as you use a safety pin to attach each organ onto the shirt. Attach it from the inside of the shirt so the safety pins can't be seen. This way, when you need to wash the shirt, it's easy to take off the organs.

7. Use a thin paintbrush to drip red fabric paint over the T-shirt for an extra gory effect.

8. When the paint is completely dry to the touch, put on the T-shirt and walk around the house mumbling, "I'm some*body*. I'm really some*body*."

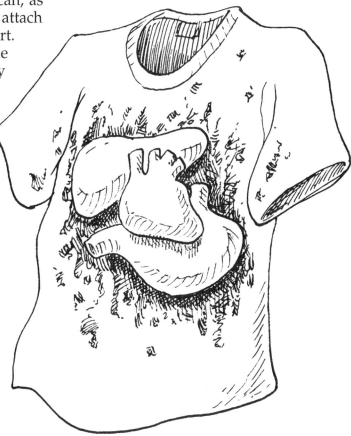

When you wear this heart-stopping hat, your friends will wonder if you're dead or alive.

ICKY INGREDIENTS

• pencil • cardboard • scissors • aluminum foil • glue • hat
• stapler • fake blood

DREADFUL DIRECTIONS

1. Draw the outline of a hatchet on a piece of stiff cardboard. The hatchet should be about 9 inches long, and the blade should be 6 inches by 4 inches. (See illustration.)

2. Cut out the hatchet. Cover the blade with aluminum foil to make it look more realistic. You may need to glue the edges of the foil to the cardboard to keep it in place.

3. Now find a hat that you don't mind cutting. Make a slit in the top of the hat as wide as the hatchet blade. Don't make the slit longer than the blade, or the blade will fall through the hat.

6"   4"   9"

4. Stick about an inch of the hatchet blade into the slit. Carefully bend that inch of blade and staple it to the inside of the hat.

5. Put on the hat, and dribble some fake blood down the side of your face and around the hatchet wound. Walk around looking dazed. After all, you've just been hit in the head with a hatchet!

26

14 SLIME-ADE STAND

Your customers won't be able to get enough of this green drink. It may look gross, but it sure tastes great!

ICKY INGREDIENTS

• black olives • ice cube tray • pitcher • limeade • lemonade • ginger ale • long-handled spoon • table and chair • clear plastic cups • poster board • pens or magic markers

DREADFUL DIRECTIONS

1. Before you make your slime-ade, freeze a batch of eyeball ice cubes to serve in the drinks. Put an olive into the center of each ice cube mold in an ice cube tray. Fill the tray with water, then put it in the freezer to freeze. You may want to fix a few trays.

2. While your eyeballs are freezing, whip up a batch of slime-ade. In a pitcher, mix equal parts of limeade, lemonade, and ginger ale. Stir it, then put it in the refrigerator to keep it cold.

3. Set up a table and chair outside your house. Using poster board and pens or magic markers, make a big sign that reads "The Grossest (but the best!) Slime-ade." Include the price per cup on the sign as well.

4. When your stand is ready for customers and your ice cubes are frozen, it's time to open for business! Bring out the pitcher of slime-ade, cups, and the ice cubes in a covered bowl or a small ice chest.

5. When a thirsty customer drops by, pour him or her a drink and top it off with a pair of eyeball ice cubes. Be prepared to mix up lots and lots of this creepy drink!

15 MONSTER MADNESS MOBILE

PARENTAL SUPERVISION RECOMMENDED
These moving monsters that sway in the wind are a breeze to make!

ICKY INGREDIENTS

• scissors •paper plate • ruler • three different colors of curling ribbon • pencil • poster board • different-colored marker pens • beads, buttons, yarn, fabric scraps • colored construction paper • glue • tape • pushpin

---

DREADFUL DIRECTIONS

1. With a parent's help, use a pair of scissors to poke six small holes evenly around the edge of a paper plate. Leave about 4 ½ inches between each hole.

2. With a ruler and scissors, cut two 12-inch pieces of curling ribbon, two 10-inch pieces of another color ribbon, and two 8-inch pieces of a third color ribbon.

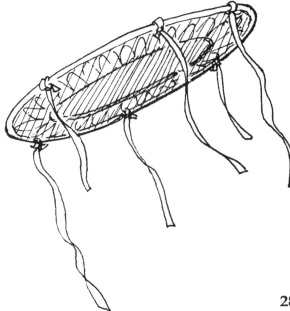

3. Tie a piece of ribbon through each hole. Don't put two strings of the same length right next to each other, or your mobile will be off balance. Let the ends of each ribbon hang down. Set the base for your mobile aside while you begin your monster madness!

4. Draw six monster heads on the poster board, then cut them out. Now let your imagination go wild! Fill the monsters' faces with three eyes, two noses, big fangs, jagged teeth, huge scars, or anything else you want. Remember to decorate both sides of each monster head. You may want to draw the front and back of each head or draw two faces on each side— *you're* the monster maker!

5. Decorate the faces further by gluing on raised buttons or beads for beastly, bugged-out eyes. Add yarn or fabric scraps for ferocious hairy faces.

6. Once your monsters are finished, poke a tiny hole in the top of each monster and tie it to a ribbon on the paper plate. If one monster face has a lot of decorations on it, position it on the plate so it is opposite another heavily decorated monster. This will help balance the mobile.

7. Poke a small hole in the center of the plate. Cut off a piece of ribbon (any color) 12 to 14 inches long, then pull 2 inches of ribbon through the hole and tape it to the plate's underside. This will be your hanging ribbon.

8. Attach the mobile to a ceiling or doorway by sticking a pushpin through the ribbon, then into the ceiling or doorway. You may need a parent, a step stool, or a very tall monster to help you hang it!

16 GREEN MONSTER FROM MARS

Pretend you're a frightening Martian who's arrived on Earth in search of human specimens.

ICKY INGREDIENTS

• colander (a metal one, preferably, with legs) • aluminum foil
• black garbage bag • scissors • belt •long-sleeved T-shirt •black
leggings or shorts • two large rubber bands • two small
aluminum foil plates • paper hole punch • green face paint

DREADFUL DIRECTIONS

1. To make your space helmet, ask a parent if you can borrow a colander from the kitchen. If the colander isn't metal, cover it with crinkled aluminum foil.

2. Twist two long sheets of aluminum foil into two antennas. Attach on either side of the colander by wrapping the antennas around the legs.

3. To make your space tunic, cut a hole for your head out of the bottom of a black garbage bag. On either side of the head hole, cut out two arm holes. If you're a fashionable Martian, add a belt around the waist. Wear your tunic over a long-sleeved T-shirt and black leggings or shorts.

4. For otherworldly protective knee pads, take two small aluminum plates. Cut two oversized rubber bands in half. Punch two holes on opposite sides of each plate, and string a rubber band through the holes on each plate. Slip the plates over your knees and tie the ends of the rubber bands together behind each knee.

5. Last but not least, paint your face and hands a ghastly green with face paint. Put on your space helmet and you're all set! You can make up your own Martian language and start babbling in it to everyone you see!

FURTHER FRIGHT

Gather some of your favorite Martian friends, and create your own Martian alphabet. You can then write notes to each other in "Martianese." If any letter falls into the wrong alien hands, your secret message is safe!

Hiding this life-sized skeleton in a closet will surely rattle somebody's bones!

ICKY INGREDIENTS

- three sheets of large white poster board • pencil • black marker
- scissors • paper hole punch • paper fasteners • white string
- coat hanger

DREADFUL DIRECTIONS

1. Draw life-sized outlines of the skeleton parts on pieces of poster board. To figure out the approximate size of each bone, use your own body as a guide. Make sure to include everything from the foot bones and shin bones to the neck bone and the head! Look in an encyclopedia for guidance.

2. With a thick black marker pen, outline each part. Then add creepy eyes, a nose hole, a sneering grin to the head, and horizontal lines for the ribs. Detail the other bones as shown.

3. Cut out all the pieces and lay them out on the floor in the form of a skeleton.

4. Use a paper hole punch to punch a hole in the ends of each joint. With paper fasteners, fasten the bone joints together in the proper order.

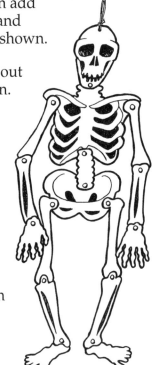

5. Punch a hole in the top of the skeleton's head, and thread a piece of white string through the hole. Tie a knot so that you can hang the skeleton.

6. Put the loop over the hook of a coat hanger. Stick the skeleton in a friend's closet or any other place you can think of, and wait for the shrieks to start!

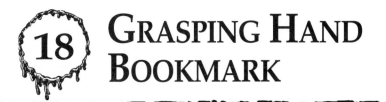

Need a helping "hand" in your reading? This ghostly bookmark will hold your place and haunt you page after page!

ICKY INGREDIENTS

• sheet of 18-by-12-inch white construction paper • pencil • scissors • black construction paper • glue • pipe cleaners

DREADFUL DIRECTIONS

1. Fold a piece of white construction paper in half widthwise. Put your hand, palm side down, on the paper, keeping your wrist on the fold of the paper. Spread your fingers. Trace the outline of your hand. Cut out the hand, making sure to cut through both layers of paper. Don't cut through the fold—the hands need to stay connected.

2. Cut five long fingernails out of black paper. Glue the fingernails onto one of the hands. Open up the hands so that one hand is lying flat (it doesn't matter which hand).

3. Poke a hole through the center of the paper fold line with a pipe cleaner. Glue the pipe cleaner along the palm and middle finger of the flat hand. Leave at least 5 inches of pipe cleaner hanging out the back of the fold. (You may need to twist the ends of two pipe cleaners together to add more length.) The 5 inches of pipe cleaner will be the bookmark—the horrible hand is the decoration.

4. Cut pieces of pipe cleaner to fit the rest of the fingers on that hand. Then glue each pipe cleaner to the correct finger.

5. Close the hands and glue them together. Bend the fingertips down to make them clawlike. Now stick the bookmark in your favorite book of ghost stories to "hold" your place!

Bust open this bat piñata and see what goodies lie in the belly of the beast!

ICKY INGREDIENTS

- large balloon • newspaper • liquid laundry starch • water
- measuring cup • small bowl • pin • assorted wrapped candies
- masking tape • black paint • paintbrush • cardboard • scissors
- glue • red and white construction paper • screw ring • string
- blindfold • stick or broom

DREADFUL DIRECTIONS

1. Blow up a balloon and tie a knot in it.

2. Papier-mâché the balloon by first tearing a few sheets of newspaper into several wide strips (approximately 1 ½ inches by 4 inches). Mix ⅔ cup starch with ⅓ cup water in a small bowl. This will be your paste. (If your balloon is large, you may need to double the recipe.) Dip an entire strip of newspaper into the bowl, and wipe off the excess paste against the side of the bowl or with your finger. Lay the wet newspaper strip on the balloon. Smooth it out, getting as many wrinkles out of the newspaper as possible. Cover the whole balloon with two layers of strips, but leave a hole around the knot that's big enough to fit the candy in. Set the balloon aside to dry.

3. Once the papier-mâché has completely dried, pop the balloon with a pin near the knot. Carefully shake out the balloon pieces through the hole.

4. Fill the papier-mâché balloon with gummy worms and other icky-looking candy, and cover the opening with masking tape.

5. Now you are ready to turn your ordinary papier-mâché balloon into a wild, bloodsucking bat! Begin by painting the piñata black. Set it aside to dry.

6. Meanwhile, you can create bat wings and ears by cutting out the four shapes from cardboard. Paint the wings and ears black, and set them aside to dry. Once everything has dried, make a ½-inch fold at the base of each wing and ear. Add glue along each fold and place on your bat's body. At this time, you may want to add big red eyes and huge white fangs, using construction paper.

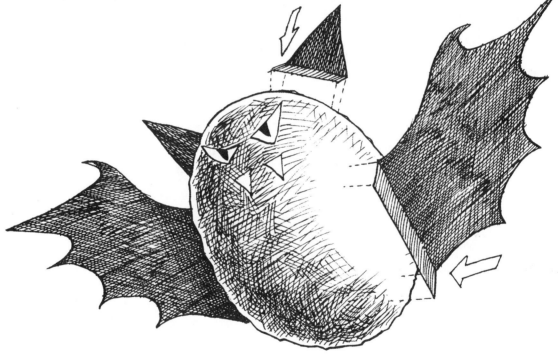

7. Carefully insert the screw ring into the middle of the piñata. Put a string through the ring to hang it. Get a parent (or a very tall friend!) to help you hang your bat from a tree in the backyard. If you don't have a tree, a swing set may work.

8. Gather your buddies, get a blindfold and a stick or broom, and take turns trying to destroy that huge, wicked bat. When you spill its guts and find the goodies inside, you'll see what a big sweet tooth this bat had!

HOMEMADE HORROR FILM

Why pay money to see a scary movie when you can screen your own homemade one?

ICKY INGREDIENTS

• empty half-gallon milk carton • scissors • clear acetate (available at art supply stores) • tape • marker pens, various colors • ruler • flashlight

DREADFUL DIRECTIONS

1. Begin by washing and drying the carton thoroughly. Cut off the top and the bottom so you have a rectangular tube for your "viewer." Cut two slits, each about 3 inches long, on opposite sides of the carton.

2. Now cut strips of acetate, each just under 3 inches wide. Tape them together into one long "filmstrip."

3. Place the filmstrip horizontally in front of you. Use a black marker to divide the acetate strip into a series of frames, each about 3 ½ inches wide.

4. Now, leaving the first couple of frames empty, draw a scene on each frame using different-colored markers. Make your pictures very simple.

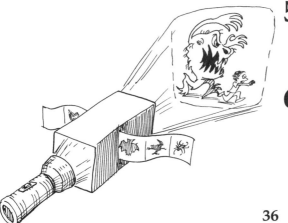

5. Slide your "filmstrip" through one slit in the carton and out the other end so that the first scene is inside the carton.

6. Turn off the lights. Shine the flashlight through an open end of the carton and onto a blank wall. The images you drew will be projected onto the wall. Pull the acetate through, frame by frame, until your horror film is over!

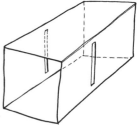

36

Your venom is deadly when you wear this killer black widow spider costume.

ICKY INGREDIENTS

- two pairs of old opaque black nylons • T-shirt • newspaper
- long black T-shirt • chalk or bright-colored marker •scissors
- black tights or black jeans • red felt

DREADFUL DIRECTIONS

1. To make a set of spider legs, stuff one pair of old nylons with newspaper. Leave about 4 inches unstuffed on each leg at the top.

2. Put a T-shirt on, so the nylons won't rub against your skin. Then tie the legs in a knot around your rib cage.

3. Repeat step 1 with the second pair of nylons. Tie it around your waist, below the first pair.

4. Put on the black T-shirt. Mark where the spider legs are with chalk or a bright-colored marker. Take off the T-shirt and cut holes where the spider legs need to poke through. Put the T-shirt back on and pull your two pairs of nylon legs through the holes. Put on the black tights or jeans. Now, counting your own arms and legs, you have eight spider legs!

5. Cut a large hourglass shape out of red felt and glue it in the middle of the T-shirt. This is the deadly red marking that identifies you as a black widow spider. Hide in a closet or just "hang around," waiting for your prey!

THE BUG FAMILY CEMETERY

Ashes to ashes, dust to dust . . . A gruesome gravesite makes the perfect resting place for your insect friends!

ICKY INGREDIENTS

• matchboxes • cotton strips or cotton balls • a 2-foot by 2-foot patch of your backyard • Popsicle sticks • glue • deceased bugs • spoon • cardboard • scissors • pen • dandelions or flowers

DREADFUL DIRECTIONS

1. Ask your parents for a few empty matchboxes. These will serve as the bugs' coffins.

2. Line each coffin with strips of cotton or wisps pulled from cotton balls so that each insect will have a comfortable resting place for all eternity (some bugs may prefer a few blades of grass instead).

3. With a parent's help (and permission!), find a small plot of land (2 feet by 2 feet) to use as a bug cemetery. Make sure the dirt is soft and easy to dig up.

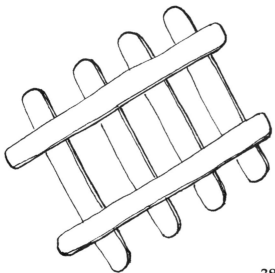

4. You'll want to fence off the graveyard so that no one will walk on top of your bugs' tombstones. To make a mini-picket fence, lay four Popsicle sticks side by side, with about ½ inch to an inch of space between each one. Then glue one Popsicle stick across the four sticks, about an inch from the top. Glue another stick across the four sticks about an inch from the bottom. (See illustration.) This will become one section of the fence.

5. Make as many fence sections as you need to encircle the entire graveyard. Push the sections into the ground, so that each one is touching the one beside it.

6. The next time you find a dead bug in the yard or on the sidewalk, give it a decent burial by placing it gently in one of the coffins. Use a spoon to dig its grave, then place the coffin in the hole and bury it.

7. Mark the grave with a "tombstone" bearing the name of your dear, departed bug. Cut out a tombstone shape from a piece of cardboard, write the insect's name on it, and stick it in the ground. Top the grave with a dandelion, or, if there are flowers in your yard, ask your parents if it's okay to pick one to put on your bug's final resting place.

Gather all of your frightful friends and put on a talent show for your neighborhood or school. You'll have your audience begging for "gore"!

ICKY INGREDIENTS

• a gang of ghoulish friends who like to perform • various props and costumes for acts • pen • paper • black construction paper • silver magic marker • an audience (not absolutely necessary)

DREADFUL DIRECTIONS

1. Gather all your friends interested in acting, singing, dancing, or reciting poetry. Ask them to prepare acts for the talent show you're producing. Request that each put a scary twist to his or her act. For example, two friends may choose to act out a bloodcurdling scene from their favorite horror film. Another may sing a sweet love song—dressed like Dracula.

2. Choose a stage. If it's just your family, the living room will do, but if it's your whole neighborhood, you may need to do it in your backyard. Set up chairs or put out blankets for everyone to sit on.

3. Stage a rehearsal to make sure everyone is ready. At that time, write down anything you may need to do during the show, such as operating the tape player or dimming the lights.

4. Make ghoulish invitations by writing down the play's details—time, date, and place—on black construction paper with a silver magic marker. Get some friends to help you distribute the invitations.

5. Sit back and enjoy the really big (and really scary) show! It's okay if you decide not to have an audience—just have fun with your friends!

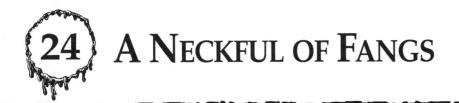

24 — A NECKFUL OF FANGS

No respectable vampire hunter should be without his or her own collection of vampire fangs to hang on a necklace.

ICKY INGREDIENTS

•1 cup flour • ¼ cup salt • ⅓ cup water • mixing bowl • mixing spoon • wax paper • rolling pin • knife • paper clips • red poster paint • paintbrush • clear nail polish • white yarn • scissors

DREADFUL DIRECTIONS

1. To make your vampire fang "charms," mix the flour, salt, and water in a bowl until it forms a doughy clay. Press the clay between your fingers to work out any lumps.

2. Put the clay onto a large piece of wax paper, and roll it out with a rolling pin. You need to spread out the dough until it's about ¼ inch thick.

 **3.** With a knife, cut out some wicked-looking fangs. Push a paper clip into the back of each fang so it is partially covered by dough. The top end should stick out ¼ inch above the charm.

4. Let the charms dry out in a dry, warm place for two or three days. Turn them once each day to make sure each charm dries evenly.

5. When they are completely dry and hard to the touch, paint on ghoulish blood with red poster paint. After the paint is dry, add a layer of clear nail polish to make the teeth shiny and the blood glisten!

6. Cut a piece of yarn long enough to fit over your head. Thread the yarn through the paper clips on the teeth. Tie the ends of the string together. The next time you see a vampire, compare teeth with him!

25 MUTANT MASK

When you're from the feared planet Meltoid, your lava-looking face will have earthlings running from you left and right.

ICKY INGREDIENTS

• dinner-size paper plate • scissors • pipe cleaners • cotton balls • stapler • red and yellow food coloring • white glue • small piece of cardboard • newspaper • string

DREADFUL DIRECTIONS

1. First, cut out some basic Meltoid features from your paper plate: two jagged nose holes, one gashed-out mouth, and three beady eyes.

2. Next, staple two curved pipe cleaners to the top of your Meltoid paper-plate face for antennas. Glue cotton balls to the ends of the antennas.

3. Now create your melted Meltoid features by mixing drops of red and yellow food coloring on a small piece of cardboard with about 3 or 4 tablespoons of glue.

4. Once you've got a glowing lava color, fold the cardboard in half and drip your Meltoid "skin" onto the mask. Put some newspaper under your work surface to catch the excess flow. Dribble the lava so that it runs down the face of the mask and down your antennas as well.

5. When your lava skin has dried, poke holes in each side of the plate and tie strings through them. Leave enough string so that you can tie the mask around your head.

6. Wear your Meltoid face around the house and growl at everyone you see.

FURTHER FRIGHT

You and your freaky friends can create a whole colony of Meltoids. Use different colored food coloring to drizzle on the masks, making different ages and races of Meltoids. Gather together and decide the fate of the errrant earthling race you have discovered! Will you melt them?

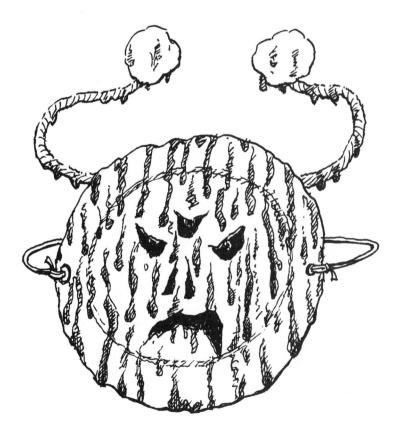

EGGS-CEPTIONALLY CREEPY CRITTERS

Turn these eggshells into witches, pumpkins, and horrible monsters for eggs-cruciating terror.

ICKY INGREDIENTS

• three or four eggs • small mixing bowl • needle • felt or construction paper, in various colors, including black • scissors • crayons or colored markers • yarn or curled ribbon • glue

DREADFUL DIRECTIONS

1. First, you will need to blow out the insides of the eggs. Here's how to do it: With the needle, make a small puncture hole in the end of the egg that will eventually serve as the top of your creature's head. Then make a hole in the other end, but don't take the needle out. Move the needle around inside the egg until the hole is about ½ inch wide. Carefully remove the needle, and hold the egg over a small bowl. Blow through the smaller hole to make the inside of the egg come out of the bigger hole. Rinse out the empty eggshell carefully with cool water. Repeat this step with each egg.

2. Once you have prepared your monsters' eggshell bodies, you are ready to add their creepy features. Cut out small pieces of felt or construction paper, and glue them on to make beady or bloodshot eyes. Use crayons or markers to add frowns or gap-toothed smiles. For wild monster hair, glue on strands of yarn or curled ribbon. Use your imagination! Keep in mind that the eggs are fragile, so use a gentle hand when applying or coloring features.

3. Make a stand for each creepy creature by cutting a strip of construction paper about 4 inches long and 1 inch high. Glue the ends together to form a circle. Let the stands dry, then rest each egg on top of them. Eggs-cellent!

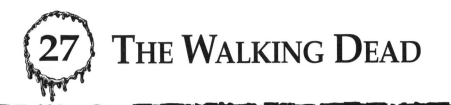

27 THE WALKING DEAD

Some people just don't know when to stay dead! After spending twenty years buried underground, you couldn't look any grosser than you do in this costume.

ICKY INGREDIENTS

• white face mask that covers your eyes and nose (available at costume stores) • jeans • T-shirt • dirt • weeds • stapler • cooked spaghetti

DREADFUL DIRECTIONS

1. Do this activity outside in your backyard, so you won't track any dirt into the house. Take the white mask and rub it in the dirt to make it look like something that's been buried for years. Try not to get dirt on the side that will be against your skin. Take an old pair of jeans and a T-shirt, and rub them in the dirt also.

2. Pull some weeds and staple them all over the front of the mask. (Make sure they're weeds and not someone's favorite plant!)

3. To create icky worms crawling around your face, cook up several strands of spaghetti with a parent's help. While they're still warm and moist, hang them through the eye holes. They should stick to the mask as they dry.

4. Put on your clothes and the mask. Stick some weeds in your hair, and hang a spaghetti worm in the corner of your mouth.

FURTHER FRIGHT

Blacken your teeth with tooth blackener (available at costume stores). After all, your pearly whites disintegrated years ago!

Put on your terrifying thinking cap and "dig up" all the ghoulish news that's fit to print!

ICKY INGREDIENTS

- several sheets of 11-by-17-inch white copier paper or butcher paper • two or three copies of daily newspapers • notepads • pencils • access to photocopy machine • plastic bags (for rainy days only)

DREADFUL DIRECTIONS

1. First, grab a friend or two and decide what sections you would like to have in your nightmare newspaper. Here are a few suggestions:

FRIGHTENING FICTION—scary "news" stories

WITCHES' BREW—food tips and recipes from cannibals and regular folk

WEREWOLF WATCH—interviews with the most happening guys and ghouls in town

VAMPIRE VACATION TIPS—hot spots where you can have a horrifyingly good time after dark

2. Next, take a look at your daily newspapers. Study how the articles are laid out on the page. Pay attention to the format of the pictures and artwork. Notice the different-sized type used in the headlines. This information will help you come up with ideas for setting up your own paper.

3. Now it's time to "sniff out" the news. Set a deadline for everyone to turn in his or her stories. Be sure that the stories are written in columns, as seen in a real newspaper. They can be typewritten, handwritten neatly, or done on a computer. Write scary, creepy, funny stories—anything goes!

4. Draw cartoons and create advertisements fit for all creatures, large and small. Don't forget to add some spooky, dramatic pictures to accompany your news articles.

5. Once you've gathered all the necessary material, you are ready to put together your first issue of *Creature Feature*. Fold your paper in half to make it 8 ½ inches by 11 inches. Now lay out your newspaper by cutting and pasting the column articles and drawings onto the folded paper. Be careful not to put anything in the newspaper fold.

6. When you have completed your pages, you're ready to photocopy your first edition. Get a parent to help you take your originals to a photocopy center.

7. With your team of "delivery ghouls," distribute *Creature Feature* to your family and friends. And if it's raining, remember to put your papers into plastic bags.

THE MOST BEAUTIFUL GHOUL IN SCHOOL

This dead prom queen costume is a cinch to make. When you wear it, you'll be the most beautiful girl—at Graveyard High, that is!

ICKY INGREDIENTS

• pretty dress, the bigger and flouncier, the better • high heels • accessories • tiara or fake jewels, glue, and a headband • white powder • black eyebrow pencil • fake blood

DREADFUL DIRECTIONS

1. Show off what a beauty you were before you were so rudely shot in the neck. Borrow an old party dress from your mom or big sister, and slip on a pair of heels. If you don't own any, ask your mom, your sister, or a friend if you can borrow a pair. (You can always stuff the toes with toilet tissue if they're too big.)

2. Add some accessories, such as dangling earrings and an exquisite necklace.

3. Fix your hair in the most feminine hairdo possible. Pile it high on your head, or if your hair is shorter, try this: Bend over, letting your head hang upside down, and apply hairspray. It will give you a full, fluffy look.

4. Top your head with a tiara. If you can't find one, you can make your own by gluing plastic jewels on a headband.

5. Powder your face with white face powder. After all, you lost all the color in your cheeks after your demise.

6. With a black eyebrow pencil, draw a hole on your neck the size of a bullet wound. Splatter fake blood around the wound and down your neck.

7. Put some fake blood at the corner of your mouth, and greet everyone you meet with a big, frozen smile. Corpses just can't be that warm!

FURTHER FRIGHT

Stage a beauty contest. Have all your friends dress up as beastly beauties and ghastly guys. Get a sibling or a parent to judge your pageant. Compete for Mr. Horror (scariest male), Miss Monstrosity (scariest female), Mr. Creepy Cadaver (grossest male), Miss Gross Guts (grossest female), Mr. Gory Goof (funniest male), and Miss Sickening-n-Silly (funniest female).

Don't forget to provide mini awards for the winners. Plastic spider rings, fake vampire teeth, and gummy worms are a few ideas. May the best ghoul win!

30 NIGHT FRIGHT

PARENTAL SUPERVISION RECOMMENDED
With these dreadful pillow decorations, you can look forward
to a good night(mare)'s sleep!

ICKY INGREDIENTS

- white pillowcase • pencil • permanent black marker • crayons
- newspapers (1-inch thick stack) • paper towels • iron

DREADFUL DIRECTIONS

1. Ask your parents for an old white or light-colored pillowcase you can keep. Put the pillowcase on a table or other hard surface. With a pencil, lightly sketch in the outline of a scary creature (or your own worst nightmare!). The design should be on only one side of the pillowcase.

2. Then, outline your picture with a permanent black marker. Color in your design with crayons. Press hard to make sure you get plenty of color on the pillowcase.

3. Fill the pillowcase with a 1-inch-thick stack of newspapers. After that, place enough paper towels over the outside design to completely cover it.

4. With a parent's help, iron the paper towels over the design for about two minutes to seal in the crayon colors permanently. As you iron the crayon into the pillowcase, the crayon will appear to attach itself to the paper towels. Stop periodically and check the paper towels. When all of your design looks like it has attached itself to the paper towels, your pillowcase should be completely ready. Remove the paper towels.

5. Once the pillowcase cools off, snuggle up with your scary bedtime beastie. And if you spill something on your creature, wash it in warm water, and your phantom friend will still be there when it comes out of the washer and dryer!

Turn yourself into a scary skeleton with this glow-in-the-dark T-shirt!

ICKY INGREDIENTS

• black T-shirt • fluorescent-colored fabric paint (available in craft stores) • paintbrush • newspapers

DREADFUL DIRECTIONS

1. First, check with your parents to make sure it's okay if you paint a design on a black T-shirt.

2. Spread out plenty of newspapers on a flat surface. Lay your T-shirt flat on the newspapers, and prepare to operate! With the fabric paint, paint a set of ribs onto the front of the T-shirt. You can add shoulder bones, too.

3. Once the T-shirt dries, turn it over and paint a long backbone as well as the backs of the ribs. Leave the T-shirt to dry until the next day. At night, turn off the lights and slip on the shirt. You'll look like a vision of death!

FURTHER FRIGHT

You can make a completely different costume using the same Icky Ingredients. How about painting a creepy spiderweb with an even creepier spider dangling from it?

It's a great gift for your favorite spider lover!

You're the perfect little angel ... until you turn around and become a little devil!

ICKY INGREDIENTS

• aluminum foil • two pipe cleaners • headband • paper plates • poster paint • paintbrush • red, white, and black construction paper • glue • paper hole punch • two rubber bands • scissors • heavy tape

DREADFUL DIRECTIONS

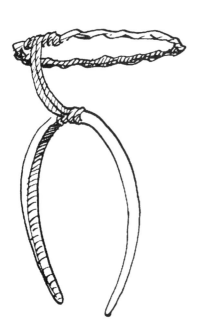

1. To become an instant angel, all you need to do is make a halo. Twist a long piece of foil into a thin ropelike shape, then bend it around to form a halo. Twist two pipe cleaners right next to each other onto the back of the halo. Then twist the other ends of the pipe cleaner to the top of the headband to attach the halo. To make the halo look like it is centered over your head, you may need to bend the pipe cleaners back slightly. (See illustration.)

2. To make a devil mask for the back of your head, paint a paper plate red. Cut eyes, nose, and a devilish grin out of black and white construction paper. Glue the facial features to the mask. Create ears out of red construction paper, and glue them onto either side of the plate.

3. With a paper hole punch, make a hole about an inch from the edge of the plate at ear level. Punch another hole on the opposite side.

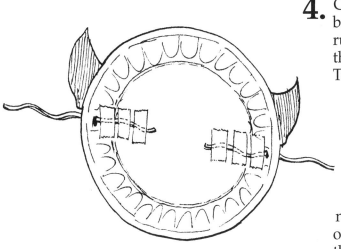

4. Cut two long rubber bands in half. Then push a rubber band halfway through one of the holes. Tape down half of the rubber band on the underside of the mask to secure it. (You may need to use several pieces of tape.) Then do this on the other side as well. You will need the untaped halves of the rubber bands to tie the mask to the headband.

5. To attach the mask to the headband, first wrap each rubber band around each end of the headband and tie each rubber band in a knot. If your rubber band is extra long, you may need to wrap it around the end of the headband a few times before tying it. Carefully put the headband on, then slip the devil mask on to the back of your head.

6. If the devil mask is sticking up too much, take it off and trim a little bit off the top. Now you're ready to be perfectly nice... or a little bit naughty!

Use this little but lethal paper kite to dive-bomb all of your enemies!

ICKY INGREDIENTS

• two 11-inch-long sticks of lightweight wood (available at hobby stores) • at least 20 feet of string • one sheet of 13-by-13-inch black construction paper • stapler • cellophane tape • scissors • a long black ribbon • white and red construction paper

DREADFUL DIRECTIONS

1. Lay the two sticks on top of each other to form a cross. To tie the sticks together, wrap 3 feet of string tightly around them. Once secure, tie a knot in the string. Let the remaining 17 feet of string hang down. This will be the string of your kite.

2. Lay the black construction paper flat on a table. Place the sticks on the center of the diamond, aligning each corner with each stick end. Fold the construction paper inward about an inch on all four sides to cover up the ends of the sticks. Carefully staple the paper right next to both sides of each stick, and put tape around the folded edge of the paper, leaving no folded edges untaped.

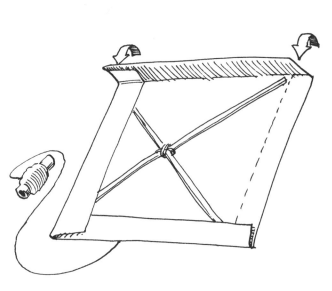

3. With scissors, punch a very small hole in the center of the kite, and pull the string through. Put tape around the hole to keep it from ripping. Now, when you fly your kite, you'll be able to see its freaky face!

4. To decorate your kite, staple a long black ribbon to the bottom of the kite. Cut out a pair of evil red eyes and a pair of big white fangs from construction paper. Glue them to the front of the kite. Now wait for a breezy day and go fly a real killer kite!

FURTHER FRIGHT

Decorate your kite with different materials. Carefully cut panels out of your kite and replace them with tissue paper or plastic wrap to make them almost see-through. You'll have to experiment to see which materials work best for your flying conditions.

You may also try sky-writing. Cut a message or your name out of a long thin piece of construction paper. Glue each letter or word separately onto the tail of the kite, and fly it for everyone to see!

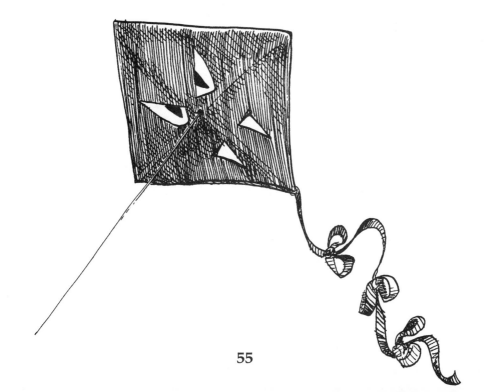

DEAD-HEAD GARDEN

It's time to stop and smell the flowers when you're in this gruesome garden filled with little human heads!

ICKY INGREDIENTS

• sixteen pipe cleaners • green marker • four egg-shaped Styrofoam balls (found at a costume or craft store) • dried-up weeds • glue • acrylic paints, in assorted colors • paintbrush • buttons and beads • yarn and pins • Styrofoam stand or vase

DREADFUL DIRECTIONS

1. Create flower stems by using a green marker to color the pipe cleaners.

2. Twist four green pipe cleaners together and stick one end into a Styrofoam ball. Repeat with four more pipe cleaners and a second Styrofoam ball. Continue until you have four flowers. Glue dried-up weeds to the stems.

3. Paint each Styrofoam head with acrylic paint. Let it dry. Apply a second coat and let that dry.

4. Paint the details of each face, including rotted teeth, hairy warts, and anything else you'd like. Make the expressions as horrible as you can.

5. Add eyeballs by gluing on buttons or beads. For hair, glue on yarn. You may want to stick a bunch of pins on the top of one head so that your dead-head's hair is literally standing on end!

6. After you've finished "growing" your flowers, put them in a vase or in a Styrofoam stand. If you choose to use a Styrofoam stand, be sure to space the flowers evenly or the stand may fall over.

FURTHER FRIGHT

Plant a little fright for your parents, and put a few of these horrifying flowers into some indoor flower pots or in amongst the flowers in the garden. Your mom and dad will freak out when they discover the frightful flowers that sprang up when they weren't looking! Who planted *those* seeds?

35 TELLING TERROR TALES

Tell chilling ghost stories that will make your blood run cold and your creativity run hot!

ICKY INGREDIENTS

• a bunch of freaky friends • a flashlight

DREADFUL DIRECTIONS

1. Gather your friends into a circle, and turn down the lights. Explain to them that everyone plays a role in telling these tales. The "terror-telling sword" (a flashlight held at chin level to light up your face) will be passed from person to person, and whoever is holding it is the only one allowed to speak. You start the game by telling the beginning of a ghost story.

Here are a few story ideas to get you started:

"I'd been floating on a raft in the ocean for days. Practically dead, I had given up all hope of ever seeing my family again. I took one last look toward the horizon, and then I saw it—a big, beautiful island. I started paddling toward it madly, when I discovered, it seemed to be paddling toward me! So, I . . ."

"I was on my way home from school, and I found myself walking by the graveyard. The wind was whipping around me so hard, it pushed me into the cemetery. Just as I turned to run away, something… or someone… grabbed my —"

"As I was eating a picnic in the park one day, a woman dressed exactly like a witch approached me. She was wearing a tall pointed black hat and a long flowing black dress. She even had a cat trailing behind her and a big gnarly wart on her nose! I almost started laughing. She didn't like that. This witch or whatever she was snarled at me, and . . ."

2. Stop at the climax, pass the terror-telling sword to the person on your left, and he or she will fill in the next part of the story, stopping at another unfinished sentence. Continue going around the circle several times to build up the story and increase the suspense, or just go around once, making sure that everyone has had a turn. The person who is last has the challenge of thinking up a great, gruesome, scary ending!

FURTHER FRIGHT

You may want to record your story on a tape recorder and play it back for the group. Does it sound creepier hearing it the second time—or goofier?

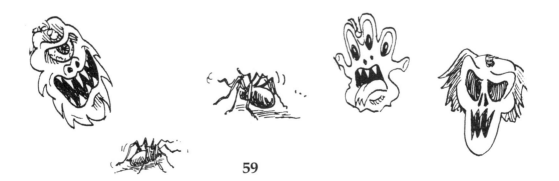

With this crazy costume, you'll become a creepy pumpkin on the prowl. You'll show those folks who have dared to scoop out your jack-o'-lantern guts!

ICKY INGREDIENTS

• large piece of orange cloth • marker • scissors • large, sturdy stapler • white chalk or pencil • wide black ribbon • black felt • fabric glue • newspaper • a large spoon or soup ladle

DREADFUL DIRECTIONS

1. To begin your pumpkin body, buy a piece of orange cloth wide enough to cover the distance from elbow to elbow with your arms extended (usually about 3 feet) and long enough to cover twice the distance from your neck to your knees (approximately 8 feet).

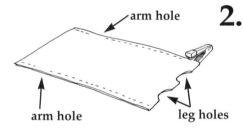

arm hole

arm hole   leg holes

2. Fold the material in half, and lay it out flat on a table. The folded side should be closest to you. Staple the sides together. Be sure to leave holes for your arms, beginning about 6 inches below the top of the material. The staples should lay right next to each other; otherwise, you will end up with unwanted holes in your pumpkin body!

3. Hold the folded material up to you, with the folded part nearest to the floor. Have a parent or brother or sister mark where your legs are. Cut two holes out of the bottom fold for your legs to fit through. Turn the sack inside out to hide the staples.

4. Near the top of the body (the side opposite the fold), cut vertical slits wide enough to fit the piece of ribbon through. The slits should be an inch apart. Thread the ribbon through the slits, going in one slit and out the other, all the way around. (See illustration.)

5. Cut out a triangular set of eyes and nose from black felt. The nose should be about 4 inches wide at the base. Also cut out a crooked, demented mouth (approximately 6 inches long). Glue the eyes, nose, and mouth onto the front of the pumpkin body with fabric glue.

6. Carefully step into the pumpkin body. Stick your legs and arms through the proper openings. Stuff the body with crumpled sheets of newspaper until it's round and full. Pull the ribbon to gather the sack at your neck and tie a bow.

7. Grab your spoon. Any time someone comes near you, wave your large spoon and scream, "How would you like to see how it feels to have your guts scooped out!"

FURTHER FRIGHT

Add a stem hat by finding a medium-sized paper sack large enough to fit snugly on top of your head. Cut leaf or petal shapes all around the open end of the bag. Decorate the leaves with green paint. Once the paint has dried, put it on!

37 CLEAN SCARY FUN

PARENTAL SUPERVISION REQUIRED
Out of a simple bar of soap, create a tombstone pencil holder to give your pencils a place to rest in peace!

ICKY INGREDIENTS

• bar of white soap • kitchen knife • scissors • pencils

DREADFUL DIRECTIONS

1. First, you need to form the shape of a horizontal tombstone. With an open pair of scissors or a knife, have a parent help you scrape the long, thin bottom of the soap to form a flat surface.

2. With the knife or scissors, carve rounded edges on the two upper corners of the tombstone, cutting off the excess soap.

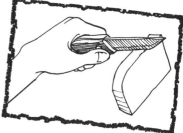

3. When you've carved your soap into the desired shape, you're ready to start chiseling! With a pencil, engrave on the front of the soap a saying, such as "Rest in Peace" or "My Pencils Lived a Good Life." At this time, you can add textured cracks with the pencil or knife.

4. Now, carefully stick a few pencils into the top of the stone, and set it on your desk or in the nearest pencil graveyard!

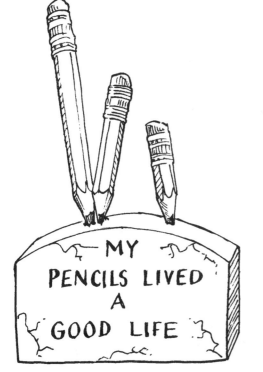

WATCH OUT, STEPHEN KING!

Become a horror thriller writer in four easy steps!

ICKY INGREDIENTS

- at least eight sheets of 8 ½-by-11-inch paper • scissors •stapler
- black pen or pencil• red marker

DREADFUL DIRECTIONS

1. Take your sheets of paper and fold them in half horizontally. Open them up and cut along the folded line.

2. Then put all your paper together and fold it in half again, so that it now looks like a small book. Open the paper up again and staple it along the fold or spine, forming your book.

3. Now you're ready to write! On a separate piece of paper, write about your worst nightmare or make up a new monster nobody has ever heard of before. When you've finished, separate the story into book pages. For instance, if you have sixteen pages in your book and your story is sixteen sentences, then put one sentence on each page.

4. Finally, you are ready to illustrate. For super thriller effects, illustrate your book with black and red pens or markers. Don't forget to name your story with a throat-grabbing title, and decorate your cover with an extra scary picture!

FURTHER FRIGHT

Do this activity with a couple of friends, and trade books for fun. They make terror-ific Halloween gifts!

The Slobbering FLESH EATER from Planet Xenon

DOGGONE SCARY MASK

Wait until you get your paws on this fang-face devilish dog mask!

ICKY INGREDIENTS

• large paper grocery bag • scissors • pencil • small lunch bag • glue • yarn • black construction paper • red felt • white construction paper • red marker pen • cotton balls

DREADFUL DIRECTIONS

1. Take a large grocery bag and cut off the top 5 inches (otherwise the mask will be too tall).

2. Put the grocery bag over your head. (Make sure that there is no writing where your face is.) With a pencil, lightly mark where your eyes are. Ask a parent or friend to help if you need it.

3. To make a scary dog snout, cut off the top 5 inches of a small paper bag. Open the bag and cut a 2-inch slit down each corner of the bag. Fold out each side to make four tabs. Attach the nose to the face by gluing the tabs onto the large grocery bag in the proper place below the eyes.

4. Cut out two large circles from black construction paper. Glue each circle where the marks for your eyes are, then cut out two small eye slits big enough to see out of. Cut out two big, black nostrils, and glue them on the end of the snout.

5. To add fur, glue brown yarn over the eyes for eyebrows and on the top of the head. Your mask will look better if you use large clumps of yarn rather than single strands.

6. Make a ferocious mouth by gluing on a long, thin piece of black construction paper on the snout, below the nostrils. Cut a wide tongue out of red felt, and glue it onto the mouth. Cut out two huge, ferocious-looking white fangs, and glue them onto the mouth on each side of the tongue. Color in the tips of the fangs with a red marker pen to make blood.

7. Put the mask on. When people approach you, give your meanest growl and watch them run!

FURTHER FRIGHT

Tear off pieces of cotton balls, and glue them to the tongue so it looks like the dog is foaming at the mouth. Not only is this devil dog scary, it has rabies as well!

SPACE-TRAVELING SPOOK

PARENTAL SUPERVISION RECOMMENDED
Did you know that ghosts from other planets are green? This quick and easy costume is out of this world!

ICKY INGREDIENTS

• old sheet • green fabric paint (available at craft stores) • pencil or white chalk • scissors • two pipe cleaners • two small Styrofoam balls (available at craft stores) • silver acrylic paint • headband

DREADFUL DIRECTIONS

1. Find a green sheet that you can cut, or with your parents' help, dye an old sheet green with the fabric paint.

2. When the sheet is dry, drape it over your head. Ask a friend to use a pencil or white chalk to mark holes for your eyes, nose, and arms. Take the sheet off, and cut out the holes. Put the sheet on again, and put your arms through the holes. Have your friend trim off the edges that drag on the floor.

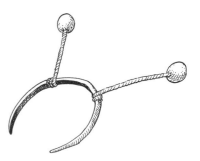

3. To make antennas, stick the end of a pipe cleaner into each Styrofoam ball. Paint the pipe cleaners and balls silver.

4. Wrap the other ends of each of the pipe cleaners around a headband so that the antennas stay secure on your head. Put the headband on over the sheet. What do green ghosts from other planets say when they want to scare someone? You decide!

41 RADIOACTIVE HORROR

You used to be so attractive ... until you were caught in the big nuclear blast!

ICKY INGREDIENTS

• face putty (available at costume stores) • liquid makeup (in your skin color) • egg carton • scissors • string

DREADFUL DIRECTIONS

1. To create a misshapen, lumpy, radioactive fallout face, knead the face putty and apply it to your face. Mold it into bumps and lumps. Don't forget to make your ears lumpy, too!

2. Spread on a layer of liquid makeup (as close to your skin color as possible) to even out the skin tone.

3. To create disfigured, eye-popping eyes, cut off two adjoining sections from an egg carton. Cut holes for your eyes in the bottom of each cup. Add some drippy putty on the cups. Poke a hole on each side, and tie strings through them. Put the "eyes" on, and tie them around your head. Lumber around the house, limping and moaning, and see the gruesome reactions you'll get!

FURTHER FRIGHT

Spray your hair with fluorescent hair paint (it washes out!) for that extra radioactive touch!

You never know what creature is going to pop up from beyond the grave in this disturbing diorama.

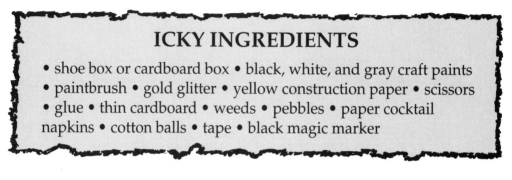

ICKY INGREDIENTS

• shoe box or cardboard box • black, white, and gray craft paints
• paintbrush • gold glitter • yellow construction paper • scissors
• glue • thin cardboard • weeds • pebbles • paper cocktail
napkins • cotton balls • tape • black magic marker

DREADFUL DIRECTIONS

1. The shoe box will be the "stage" for your graveyard. To start, paint the bottom inside of the box black. While the paint is still wet, sprinkle on some gold glitter for stars. Cut a large full moon out of yellow construction paper. Glue it on after the paint dries.

2. Stand up the shoe box on one of its long sides. Now you're ready to create your graveyard. To make a tombstone, cut out a tombstone shape from a piece of cardboard, and paint it gray. After it dries, write a heading on it. Bend the base of the tombstone back ½ inch to form a tab. Glue the tab to the bottom of the box. You'll need to make a few tombstones to fill your scene.

3. Add more "life" to your graveyard by gluing in weeds for trees and pebbles for rocks onto the bottom of the box.

4. Make your cemetery h-h-haunted by adding ghosts. First, take a paper napkin. Open it up and center it over your index finger. Fold it down around your finger, then carefully take your finger out, holding the napkin with your other hand to keep the tubelike shape. Stick a few cotton balls into the top of the shape and twist it closed. This is your basic ghost.

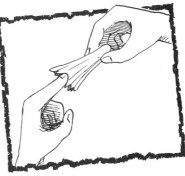

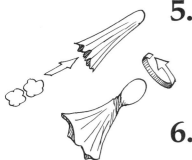

5. Put a thin piece of tape around the ghost's neck, and decorate its face with a black marker. Stick it on the back of the graveyard, in the middle of trees, or behind a tombstone. You can make as many ghosts as you want.

6. Tear apart several cotton balls, and spread the pieces on the ground and in the trees to give your graveyard a foggy, eerie atmosphere. Add whatever other creepy things you can think of. Once your diorama is complete, rest assured you've created the most chilling cemetery in the world!

PARENTAL SUPERVISION RECOMMENDED
You can really get your head into this kind of "thinking cap."

ICKY INGREDIENTS

• baseball cap or plain hat • pair of clear plastic gloves • scissors
• cotton balls • needle • red thread • fake blood (available at a costume shop) or red food coloring

DREADFUL DIRECTIONS

1. Find an old cap or hat that's okay for you to "operate" on. Ask a parent for a pair of clear plastic gloves (the kind used for dyeing hair works well), or buy some at a pharmacy. These will be the "brains" on your cap.

2. Turn the gloves inside out to give the brains a moist, shiny look. Cut off the fingers on one glove. On the other glove, cut out a large section of the palm.

3. Take the piece of the palm you cut out, crinkle it up, and with red thread, stitch "brain channels" into it. Stuff it with cotton balls, and sew it onto the cap.

4. Now stuff the cut glove fingers with cotton balls, crinkle them up to make them look like thick noodles, and sew them onto the side of the hat. Have some hang down from underneath the cap for an extra-gory effect.

5. Splatter fake blood or red food coloring all over your brains. Make sure some of the fake blood drips down your face!

44 SCARE-DY-CAT

Your friends will be the real scaredy-cats when you show up wearing this hand-held, purrfectly frightful cat mask.

ICKY INGREDIENTS

- black stockings or a pair of black nylons • scissors • coat hanger
- six pipe cleaners • black marker • glue • glitter

DREADFUL DIRECTIONS

1. Hold the coat hanger by the curved "handle" (the part that hangs on the rod). Bend the bottom of the coat hanger into a round shape that resembles the face of a cat.

2. Cut the black stockings in half, then pull one stocking half completely over the hanger. Once you've pulled it on, you may need to reshape your cat face a little.

3. Tie the stocking in a knot at the handle. Now you have the beginning of your cat mask: The nylon part is the face, and the handle is the mask holder.

4. To make a pair of ears, cut the remaining stocking in half. Carefully poke a hole in the right top side of the mask about an inch away from the edge. Thread one of the pieces of stocking through the hole, and tie it onto the mask. Repeat for the left-hand side of the mask.

5. For whiskers, color in the pipe cleaners with a black magic marker pen. Then glue them onto the middle of the mask so that they poke out.

6. To make glittery eyes, nose, and mouth, outline these features on your mask with glue. Then sprinkle the glitter directly onto the glue. Do this quickly before the glue dries. Your hand-held cat mask is ready to be worn!

45 CREEPY COCKROACH

PARENTAL SUPERVISION RECOMMENDED
With this bug beanbag, you'll be the proud owner of the biggest, grossest cockroach in town!

ICKY INGREDIENTS

• sheet of large tracing paper • pencil • scissors • two pieces of 8-by-11-inch brown cloth • straight pins • one piece of 8-by-11-inch brown felt • needle and thread • dry pinto beans • glue • buttons • white felt

DREADFUL DIRECTIONS

1. First, draw a big, ugly cockroach body (no legs) on the tracing paper.

2. Cut out your cockroach pattern. Place one piece of brown cloth on top of the other, and lay the pattern on top. Attach the pattern to the cloth with straight pins.

3. Cut out your cockroach outline from the brown cloth. This will give you two cockroach shapes. Now take the pins out, and lay your tracing paper pattern aside.

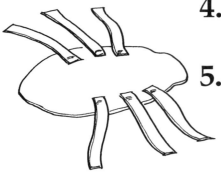

4. To make the legs, cut six strips of brown felt. Make each strip ½ inch wide and about 6 inches long.

5. Lay one cockroach shape on your worktable. Position three legs on one side of the cockroach shape and the remaining legs on the other side. (See illustration.) Sew the ends of the legs onto the pattern about ¼ inch from the edge. You may want to get a parent or older brother or sister to help you.

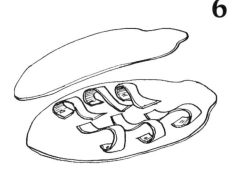

6. Gather the free ends of the legs into the center of the circle. Lay the second cockroach shape over the first. Sew the two patterns together about ¼ inch from their edges. Leave a 2- to 4-inch hole at the top of the cockroach. It may look like you're covering up the legs permanently, but you're not!

7. Turn the cockroach inside out. See how the legs fall into place? Now stuff the cockroach with dry pinto beans. Sew up the hole to keep the beans from falling out. You may want to glue on button eyes or long, sharp fangs made from white felt. Your creepy cockroach is complete!

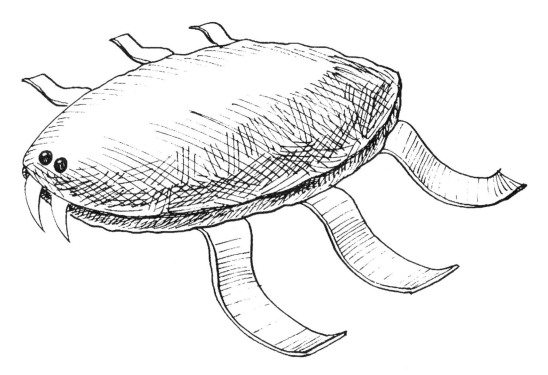

46 SPOOK SOUP

Serve up some scares by inviting your friends over to play this spine-tingling "name that ghost part" game.

ICKY INGREDIENTS

• a few pots • various props (see below) • paper and pencil

DREADFUL DIRECTIONS

1. Ask your parents if you can use a few pots. Now gather the "body parts" of a dead ghost and put each part into its own pot. Here are some suggestions:

- for eerie eyes, use peeled grapes
- for a craggy nose, use a small carrot
- for terrifying teeth, use candy corn
- for gooey brains, use cooked spaghetti
- for ghastly fat, use gelatin
- for horrible veins, use thin, wet rope
- for icky intestines, use raw hot dogs
- for killer kidney stones, use pebbles

Add any other gross body parts you can think of.

2. Gather a group of brave friends. Tell them that in the pots are the remains of a ghost. Each person must reach into the pots and try to identify the body part in each pot. Keep score by giving each person one point for each correct match.

3. After everyone has had a turn, announce the winner, then empty out the pots and let everyone see what they were really touching!

FURTHER FRIGHT

After you've played Spook Soup, how about actually making it? Pour all the edible body parts into one large pot and stir. Who dares to take the first bite?

47 THE BASIC "DRAC"

"I bid you welcome ..." You'll be the vampire host with the most in this classic Dracula costume!

ICKY INGREDIENTS

• dark pants, socks, and shoes • white dress shirt • dark bow tie or clip-on tie • one large black plastic bag • scissors • masking tape • hair gel • white face powder • black eye pencil • red lipstick • fangs (available at costume stores)

DREADFUL DIRECTIONS

1. Put on the dark pants, socks, and shoes. Next, put on the white dress shirt (your dad may have one you can borrow). If you don't have a dress shirt, any white shirt with a collar will work. Put on the bow tie around the shirt collar.

2. To make a quick 'n' easy vampire cape, unfold the black plastic bag. Spread out the bag on a flat surface with the open end facing you. Hold down one side of the bag with your hand. In the middle of the bag, cut a line all the way to the top. (Just cut through one layer of the bag, not both.) Now you have what looks like a hospital gown with a slit down the middle. Pull the bag over your shoulders, with the slit in front. Now you have an instant cape! Tie a knot in the front using the cape. If it doesn't reach around your neck, just stretch the plastic!

3. For vampire hair, slick back your hair with hair gel. Next, powder your face white to get that just-dead look. Use a black eye pencil to make your brows bushy and scary.

4. For bloodred lips, first color your lips with black eye pencil, then add a layer of bright red lipstick. For the finishing touch, don't forget a pair of fangs!

48 BAT ATTACK HAT

This creature will drive your friends batty with fear! All you have to do is tip your hat, and the bat will "fly" out and hover above your head.

ICKY INGREDIENTS

• black construction paper • white chalk or crayon • scissors • bobby pin • cellophane tape • white paper • glue • red and yellow markers • needle • 2 feet of black thread • any hat with a brim

DREADFUL DIRECTIONS

1. With a white crayon or chalk, draw the outline of a bat on black construction paper. The bat should be about 5 inches long. (If you make it too big, it won't fit under your hat.) Cut out the bat outline.

2. Bend the legs of a bobby pin out to form a small hump, which will be the hook on the bat. (See illustration.)

3. Tape the bobby pin legs securely on the back side of the bat. The hook should be sticking out from the bat's back.

4. Cut a pair of fangs and beady eyes out of white paper, and glue them on the front of the bat (the side without the hook). Draw a little blood on the fangs with a red marker, and use a yellow marker to make the eyes glow!

5. Bend the bat wings forward a bit to make the bat look more three-dimensional. Set the bat aside.

6. Thread a needle with about 2 feet of black thread. Gather both ends to create a 12-inch double thread. Tie a knot in the end. Sew a few stitches into the top of the inside of your hat, so that the end of the thread is attached to the hat and the rest of the thread hangs down. Tie a knot to hold the stitches in place. Cut off the needle. The thread should hang down about 9 or 10 inches.

7. Now grab your bat and tie the long end of the thread to the bobby pin hook. The bat should hang down about 5 or 6 inches below the brim (bottom) of the hat.

8. Carefully tuck the bat into the hat and put the hat on your head. Rush to tell your friends all about the bat invasion in your city. To prove your point, all you have to do is lift your hat!

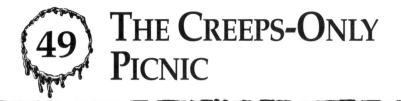

THE CREEPS-ONLY PICNIC

So you want to put together the scariest picnic ever? Organize a bash in your backyard with your favorite monsters and scary foods.

ICKY INGREDIENTS

• large blanket • picnic basket (with serving utensils and kitchenware) • various food items (see below)

DREADFUL DIRECTIONS

1. Get your parents' permission, and invite some of your favorite beasts and ghouls over for a scary nighttime picnic in your backyard.

2. Set up a large blanket for everyone to sit on. Pack a picnic basket with an array of frightening foods. Here are some suggestions to make your picnic so scary even ants wouldn't dare come!

• Put potato chips in a bowl and dribble some ketchup on them. Then ask your friends if they dare to eat skin peelings with clotted blood!

• Make soft bones (with a crunch!) with white bread, extra crunchy peanut butter, and strawberry jelly. Trim off the bread crusts, then spread on a thin layer of peanut butter, then jelly. Roll the bread into a cylinder shape, and press tightly to keep its shape. Don't squeeze too tightly, or some bone marrow (peanut butter) and blood (jelly) may squirt out!

• Bring a thermos of red fruit drink with a couple handfuls of raisins dropped in. Explain that you can't figure out how those bugs got in their drinks!

3. On this creepy picnic, anything goes! You can concoct all sorts of frightening treats using your own favorite foods.

What's that in the window? A "stained-glass" picture of a hideous witch!

ICKY INGREDIENTS

- black marker • white typing paper • crayons • aluminum foil
- rag • vegetable oil • paper towel • cellophane tape

DREADFUL DIRECTIONS

1. Using a black marker, draw the outline of a witch on a sheet of typing paper. Create an ugly witch, a terrifying witch, or any other kind of witch that you want shining through your window. Color the witch with crayons.

2. Lay a sheet of foil on your worktable. Turn over the witch drawing and lay it face down on top of the foil.

3. Dip the rag in vegetable oil. (You won't need very much.) Rub the oil over the witch. You will be able to see the drawing through the paper. Be sure to keep the vegetable oil inside the witch outline.

4. Using a paper towel, wipe off any excess oil. (The drawing will still be a little greasy to the touch, but that's okay!)

5. Tape the piece of paper to a window. When the sunlight shines through the window, the witch will look just like a transparent piece of stained glass.

FURTHER FRIGHT

Every witch has a creepy collection of frightful friends! Create other spooky "stained-glass" creatures such as vampires, monsters, and ghosts, and hang them alongside your witch.

Now It's Your Turn!

You've created monsters from paper bags and garbage bags, made bloody gifts from material scraps and red paint, frightened your friends with terrifying stories, and discovered many other ways to freak out pals and family members.

But, as you may already know, the scariest things you can create come from your imagination. So, using the various techniques you've learned in this book, create your very own super scary craft! Glow-in-the-dark cobwebs painted on a dark shirt? A papier mâché UFO spaceship? A flying bat mobile?

How scary is super scary? You decide!